D0536244

Snowy
Flowy
Blowy

Winter

Spring

A TWELVE MONTHS RHYME

BASED ON AN OLD POEM BY GREGORY GANDER

SCHOLASTIC INC.

NEW YORK TORONTO LONDON AUCKLAND SYDNEY
MEXICO CITY NEW DELHI HONG KONG

Copyright © 1999 by Nancy Tafuri. • All rights reserved. • Published by Scholastic Inc. SCHOLASTIC and associated logos are trademarks and/or registered trademarks of Scholastic Inc. • No part of this publication may be reproduced in whole or in part, or stored in a retrieval system, or transmitted in any form or by any means, electronic, mechanical, photocopying, recording, or otherwise, without written permission of the publisher. For information regarding permission, write to Scholastic Inc., Attention: Permissions Department, 555 Broadway, New York, NY 10012. • Text based on poem titled "The Twelve Months," by Gregory Gander (also known as George Ellis), from <u>The Third Treasury of the Familiar</u>, ed. Ralph L. Woods, Macmillan, 1970. The poet lived 1745-1815 • ISBN 0-439-26770-6 • 12 11 10 9 8 7 6 5 4 3

2 3 4 5/0 • The artwork was created with watercolors. • Designed by Marijka Kostiw. Handlettering by Bernard Maisner. • The text was set in Trajan Bold and Goudy. • Printed in the U.S.A.   14
First Scholastic paperback printing, December 2000

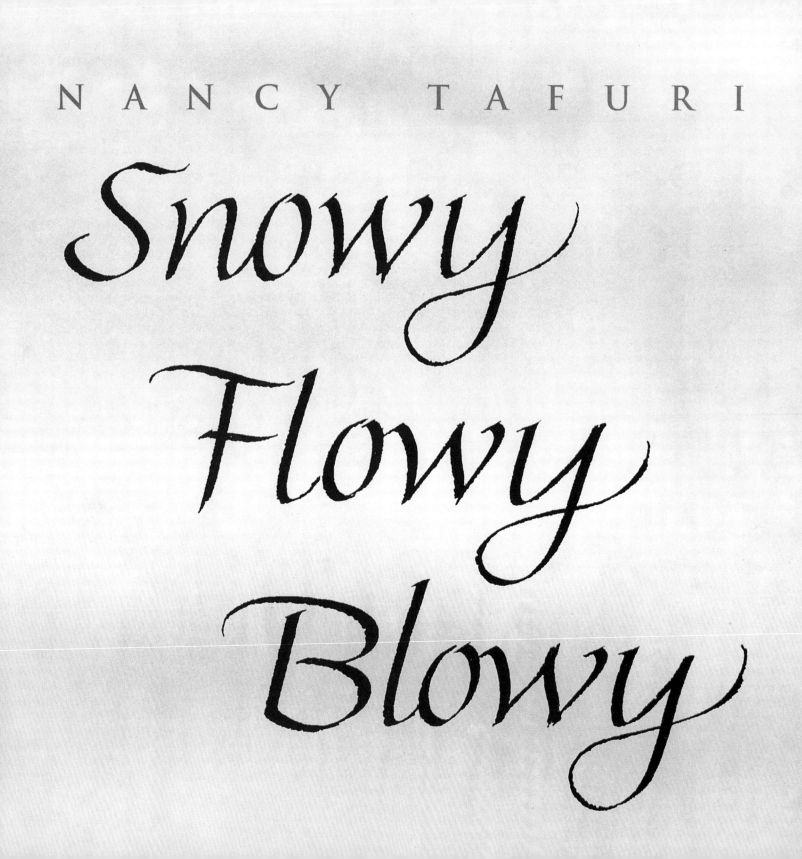

NANCY TAFURI

Snowy
Flowy
Blowy

JANUARY

Snowy

FEBRUARY

Blowy.

APRIL

Showery

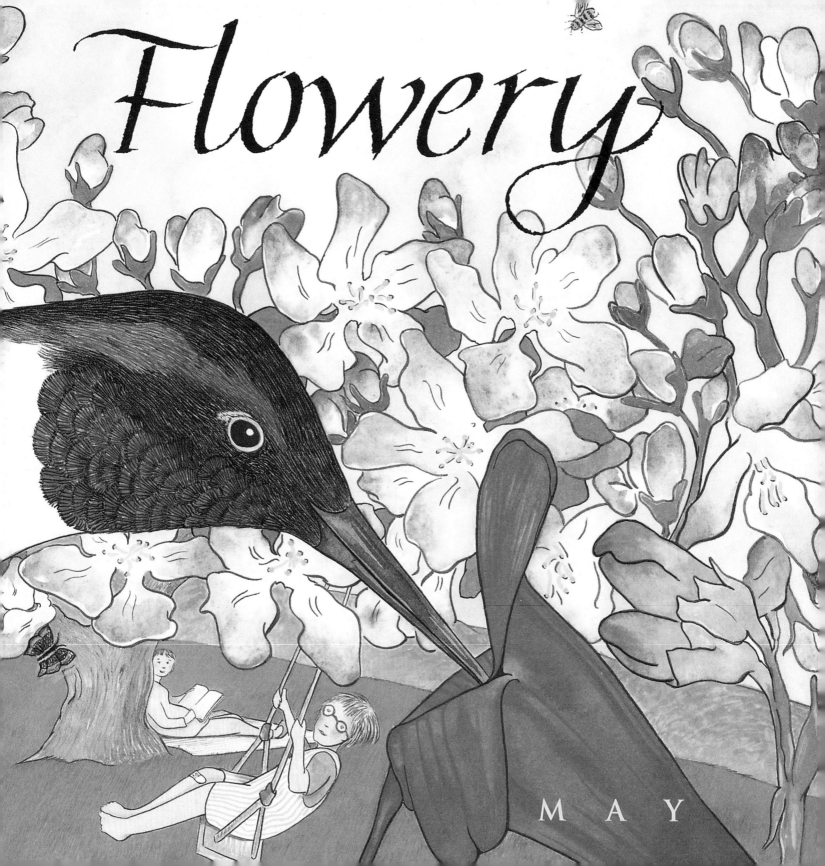

JUNE

Bowery

Hoppy

JULY

A U G U S T

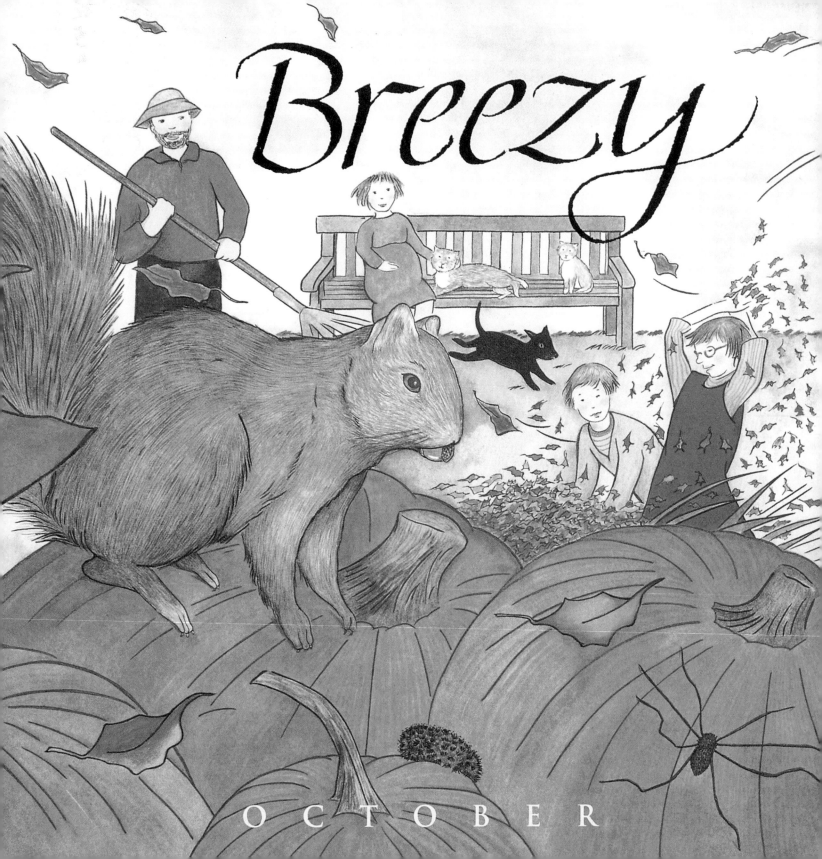

Breezy

OCTOBER

NOVEMBER

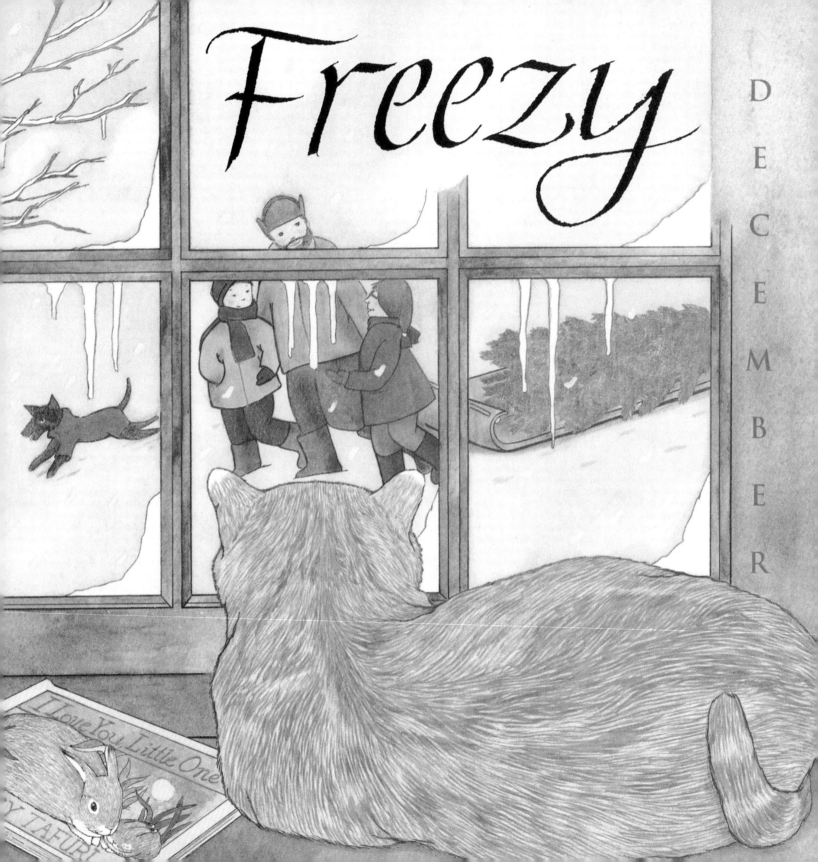

Freezy

DECEMBER

Summer

Autumn

Nancy Tafuri captured the seasonal changes of her own country neighborhood in the paintings for this book. Ms. Tafuri is the much-loved creator of more than thirty books for young children, including the Caldecott Honor Book, *Have You Seen My Duckling?* and *I Love You, Little One*. She lives in Roxbury, Connecticut, with her husband and their daughter, Cristina.